A Note from
Mary Pope Osborne About the

When I write Magic Tree House® adventures, I love including facts about the times and places Jack and Annie visit. But when readers finish these adventures, I want them to learn even more. So that's why we write a series of nonfiction books that are companions to the fiction titles in the Magic Tree House® series. We call these books Fact Trackers because we love to track the facts! Whether we're researching dinosaurs, pyramids, Pilgrims, sea monsters, or cobras, we're always amazed at how wondrous and surprising the real world is. We want you to experience the same wonder we do—so get out your pencils and notebooks and hit the trail with us. You can be a Magic Tree House® Fact Tracker, too!

Mary Pope Osborne

Here's what kids, parents, and teachers have to say about the Magic Tree House® Fact Trackers:

"They are so good. I can't wait for the next one. All I can say for now is prepare to be amazed!" —Alexander N.

"I have read every Magic Tree House book there is. The [Fact Trackers] are a thrilling way to get more information about the special events in the story." —John R.

"These are fascinating nonfiction books that enhance the magical time-traveling adventures of Jack and Annie. I love these books, especially *American Revolution*. I was learning so much, and I didn't even know it!" —Tori Beth S.

"[They] are an excellent 'behind-the-scenes' look at what the [Magic Tree House fiction] has started in your imagination! You can't buy one without the other; they are such a complement to one another." —Erika N., mom

"Magic Tree House [Fact Trackers] took my children on a journey from Frog Creek, Pennsylvania, to so many significant historical events! The detailed manuals are a remarkable addition to the classic fiction Magic Tree House books we adore!" —Jenny S., mom

"[They] are very useful tools in my classroom, as they allow for students to be part of the planning process. Together, we find facts in the [Fact Trackers] to extend the learning introduced in the fictional companions. Researching and planning classroom activities, such as our class Olympics based on facts found in *Ancient Greece and the Olympics*, help create a genuine love for learning!" —Paula H., teacher

MAGIC TREE HOUSE® FACT TRACKER

Baseball

A NONFICTION COMPANION TO MAGIC TREE HOUSE #29:
A Big Day for Baseball

BY MARY POPE OSBORNE
AND NATALIE POPE BOYCE

ILLUSTRATED BY CARLO MOLINARI

A STEPPING STONE BOOK™
Random House 🏠 New York

Library of Congress Cataloging-in-Publication Data is available upon request.
ISBN 978-1-101-93642-9 (trade pbk.) — ISBN 978-1-101-93643-6 (lib. bdg.) — ISBN 978-1-101-93644-3 (ebook)

Printed in the United States of America

10 9 8 7 6 5 4 3 2 1

This book has been officially leveled by using the F&P Text Level Gradient™ Leveling System.

336140802232548

To William DelSoldato (Coach Del),
with many thanks

Baseball Consultant:

CASSIDY LENT, reference librarian, National Baseball Hall of Fame and
Museum

Education Consultant:

HEIDI JOHNSON, language acquisition and science education specialist,
Bisbee, Arizona

Special thanks to the wonderful team at Random House: Mallory Loehr, Jenna
Lettice, Maya Motayne, Jason Zamajtuk, Carlo Molinari for the exciting art,
and as always and forever, gratitude to Diane Landolf, an editor worth her
weight in autographed baseballs

BASEBALL

Contents

Dear Readers,

In <u>A Big Day for Baseball,</u> we headed to the baseball field with Jackie Robinson. Since we were pretending to be batboys, we learned a lot about this great game. We also found out about Jackie and his early days as one of the first African Americans to play Major League Baseball. Despite trouble with people who thought that black players shouldn't be playing with white players, Jackie earned the fans' respect and became a baseball superstar.

But we had questions about baseball. How did the game get started

in the United States? What are the rules, and who are other baseball heroes? To find out, we had to track the facts. We found out that lots of the most famous players came from poor homes and climbed to the top in a game they loved.

So grab a bat, ball, and glove, and let's play ball!

Jack

Annie

1

Baseball

Baseball is often called America's national pastime. That is because baseball fans all over the country love to play and watch this great game. They think baseball is the best sport in America . . . and maybe in the whole world!

Baseball began in the United States more than 200 years ago. The game became very popular, and people have been playing it ever since. Today, grandparents, parents, and children still watch this summer sport together, and families often bring out their balls and bats at picnics and other outdoor gatherings.

Baseball is for everyone—men, women, boys, and girls. People don't need to spend a lot of money on equipment or fancy uniforms. All they need are a ball, a bat, a glove, something to mark the bases with, and a space big enough to hit a ball.

There are Little League teams in more than 80 countries around the world.

About 12 million people all across the country play on baseball teams. Over two million kids are on Little League teams worldwide. Every year there's a Little League World Series. Millions watch it on TV, and thousands of fans go to the games.

Around the World

Baseball is also a big sport in Japan, Cuba, Taiwan, Venezuela, and South Korea. There are 124 countries in the International Baseball Federation. There is even a World Baseball Classic tournament.

Players from other countries often play on teams in the United States. Many come from Latin American countries like the Dominican Republic, Venezuela, and Cuba.

Alex Rodriguez is a Dominican American baseball star who played for 22 seasons.

The Game

In baseball, there are two teams of nine players each. A baseball field has three bases and a home plate. To score a run,

16

a player tries to hit the ball with the bat, run around all three bases, and get to home plate. The team with the most runs wins.

The teams take turns batting. The team that is not batting plays on the field.

Players on the field are called <u>fielders</u>. Mookie Betts plays right field for the Boston Red Sox.

The fielding team's job is to stop the team up at bat from going around the bases. Fielders try to get the batters and runners out. After three outs, the teams switch places. The team on the field bats, and the other team plays the field.

A baseball scoreboard shows what's going on in the game.

There is no time limit for a baseball game. It lasts for nine *innings*. An inning is when both teams have had a chance to bat. If there is a tie, they play extra innings.

There are four main ways a batter or runner can be out.

Strikeout

A pitcher throws a ball that the batter tries to hit. If the batter swings and misses, it's

But a foul ball is never the third strike. Batters have been known to hit thirteen foul balls or more in one at bat.

a strike. If the batter does not swing but the umpire says the pitch was in the *strike zone*, it's a strike. If the batter hits a ball out of bounds, it's a foul ball, and that is also a strike. Three strikes, and the batter is out!

chest

strike zone

knees

The <u>strike zone</u> is the area over home plate between the batter's knees and chest.

20

If a pitch is not in the strike zone and the batter doesn't swing at it, it's called a ball. After four balls, the batter gets to go to first base. This is called a *walk*.

Fly Out

If a fielder catches a batted ball in the air before it touches the ground, the batter is out. Even if it's a foul ball, a fielder can catch it for an out. A ball hit high up into the outfield is called a *fly ball*. A ball that goes high up but only reaches the infield is called a *pop-up* or a *pop fly*.

Tag Out

After a batter makes it to a base, he becomes a runner. If a runner is not touching a base and a fielder *tags* him—or touches him with the ball—the runner is out.

Force Out

There can be only one runner on a base at a time. Imagine that a runner is already on first base. When the batter hits the ball, she must run to first base. The runner on first base can't stay there. She has to try to run to second base. This means there is a *force* at second base.

When there is a force at second base, if a fielder stops the ball, he can throw it to his

teammate at second base. If the teammate has one foot on the base and catches the ball before the runner gets there, the runner is out. This is a *force out*.

Because the batter has to try to get to first base, there is always a force at first. So an infielder can always throw the ball to first base to get the batter out.

If there's time, a fielder might force a runner out on one base, then quickly throw to another base for a second force out. That is called a *double play*. Any time there are two outs from a single pitch, it's a double play.

Hits

When a batter hits the ball and makes it to a base, it's a hit. If she gets to first base, that hit is called a single. If the batter gets to second base, it's a double. If she gets to third, it's a triple. If a batter hits the ball so far that she can run all the way around the bases and get to home plate without being tagged, it's a home run.

If a player hits a home run when the bases are loaded, meaning there are runners on all three bases, it's called a grand slam!

Turn the page to find out about the positions on a baseball field!

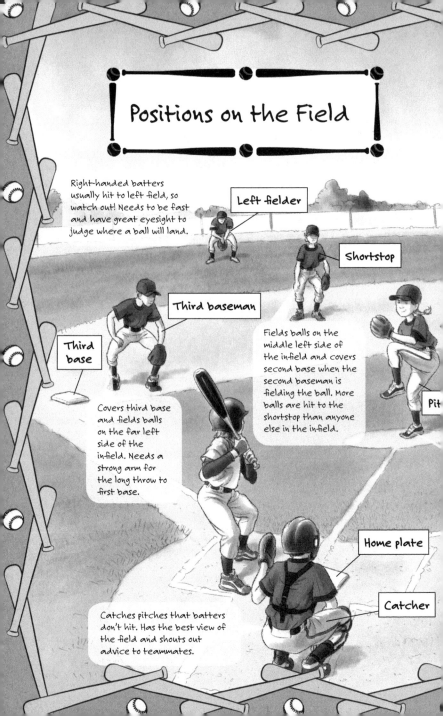

Positions on the Field

Right-handed batters usually hit to left field, so watch out! Needs to be fast and have great eyesight to judge where a ball will land.

Left fielder

Shortstop

Third baseman

Third base

Fields balls on the middle left side of the infield and covers second base when the second baseman is fielding the ball. More balls are hit to the shortstop than anyone else in the infield.

Covers third base and fields balls on the far left side of the infield. Needs a strong arm for the long throw to first base.

Pit

Home plate

Catcher

Catches pitches that batters don't hit. Has the best view of the field and shouts out advice to teammates.

...ys the farthest
...ay from home plate.
...ers a lot of ground
...must be a great
...ner who can throw
...lly far.

Stays ready for left-handed batters. Needs a strong arm to throw all the way to third base.

Center fielder

Second baseman

Right fielder

...cond
...se

First baseman

Fields balls on the middle right side of the infield between first and second. Covers second base when the ball is hit to the left side of the field.

First base

...ws the ball to batters and
...to strike them out. Also
...s first base when the first
...man is fielding the ball.

Covers first base and fields balls on the far right side of the infield. Stretches way out to catch the ball before the runner gets to first.

2

History of Baseball

Games with balls and bats have been around for a long time. About 3,500 years ago, the ancient Egyptians wrote about playing "hit catch" with bats, balls, and bases!

In the 1600s, settlers sailed from England to live in America. They brought an English game called *rounders* with them. They played it with a ball, a bat, and four posts that were like bases.

This 1897 illustration shows British naval officers playing rounders on the island of Crete.

There are stories that George Washington and his soldiers played rounders at Valley Forge. But as years passed, the old English game of rounders turned into the new American game of baseball.

The game became so popular that in 1791 the town of Pittsfield, Massachusetts, had to make a rule that people couldn't play baseball near the town's meetinghouse. This was to prevent broken windows.

Abraham Lincoln played baseball with his kids on the White House lawn!

After a hard day's work, people all over the country still relax by getting together for a game. On steamy summer nights in small towns, if you see bright lights somewhere, they are probably lighting up a baseball field.

 American soldiers have even brought baseball to Afghanistan, where they coach local kids.

The Knickerbockers

In 1845, the Knickerbockers were a baseball team in New York City. Their name came from early Dutch settlers who lived there. Dutchmen wore pants that came down to just below their knees. These pants were called knickerbockers, or knickers for short.

Most of the Knickerbockers were rich and played for fun. They wore straw hats and long pants when they played.

Making Rules

Ever since 1872, baseballs have been the same weight and size.

At first, different baseball teams followed different rules. The Knickerbockers decided to make some rules for everyone to use.

One of the new rules was that a player couldn't tag out a runner by throwing a ball at him. This was called soaking. It's a good thing they made this rule. Teams had begun using balls that were harder and faster than the balls they'd been playing with before.

First Official Game

In 1846, the Knickerbockers played the first official baseball game in history. It was official because the teams played with an agreed-upon set of rules and recorded the score.

34

By the 1850s, baseball teams were on the lookout for good players from other clubs. They offered them money to come play on their teams. In 1869, the Cincinnati Red Stockings became the first *professional* (pro-FESH-uh-nul) team in the United States.

Professional players earn money for playing.

Cincinnati Red Stockings

Today there are thirty top professional teams. They are organized into groups called leagues. Fifteen teams are

There are also hundreds of professional minor league and independent league teams all over the country.

in the American League; fifteen are in the National League. Together, they make up Major League Baseball (MLB).

The Season

The Major League Baseball season lasts from April until the end of September. Each team plays 162 games, for a total of 2,430 MLB games during the season.

The longest game ever was in 1984. The Milwaukee Brewers and the Chicago White Sox played late into the night, but the game still wasn't finished. The teams came back to finish the next day. In total, the game lasted eight hours and six minutes.

Players get a few months to rest after the season. In February, they report to spring training camps in Arizona and

Florida to practice and get back in shape.

Fans have waited all winter for the season to begin. Opening day is normally the first week in April. For over 100 years, it's been a custom that the president of the United States usually throws out the first pitch.

Baseball players are often called the boys of summer.

Barack Obama

 Teams have had batboys since the 1800s.

Batgirls and Batboys

Batboys have been with teams since the 1800s. Today there are also batgirls. If you see kids in team uniforms picking up bats on the field, they're probably batboys or batgirls. They have lots of different jobs to make the players' lives easier. One of the most important is to pick up bats that players drop on the field. They also take care of the uniforms and clean cleats and helmets.

Kids must be at least fourteen years old to get this job.

Before a game starts, batboys and batgirls stock the dugout with water and snacks. They also rub the balls with mud from a riverbank in New Jersey. This mud makes the balls easier to see and hold.

Before and after the team leaves the clubhouse, the kids tidy up and fold towels. Sometimes they even wash the players' cars or bring them pizza!

The Fans

Baseball fans love their home team. They wear their team's baseball caps and shirts. Sometimes they paint their bodies in the team's colors and travel many miles to see the games. Some super loyal fans even get tattooed with their team's name.

These Detroit Tigers fans wear tiger hats on opening day.

If you go to an MLB game, it might be a good idea to take earplugs. Some stadiums, like Dodger Stadium in Los Angeles, hold over 50,000 fans. When the fans cheer, sing, chant, and yell, the noise level is amazing ... louder than if you stood right under a giant jet that was taking off!

Baseball Food
Baseball fans eat a lot of hot dogs and sausages during a game. In just one

This is a hot dog stand at Fenway Park in Boston.

season, they can wolf down over 21 million hot dogs and 5 million sausages. Babe Ruth,

If we made a trail of all the hot dogs that baseball fans ate in one season, it would stretch from North Carolina to California!

California

a famous baseball player, sometimes ate so
many hot dogs, he'd be too full to play!

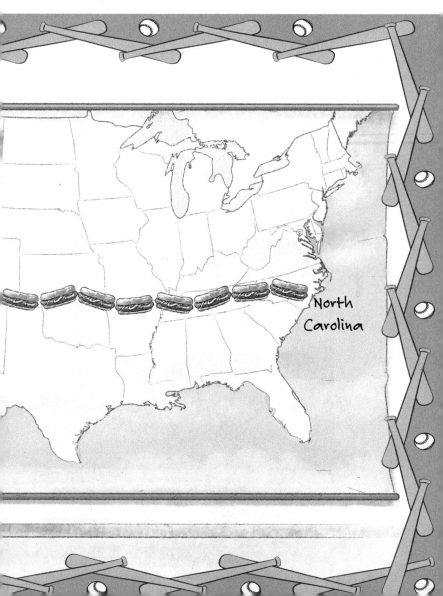

North
Carolina

The first
World Series
was in 1903.

The World Series

When the baseball season and playoffs are over in October, the two best teams play a series of games for the champion-ship. These games are called the World Series.

The New York Yankees have won the World Series twenty-seven times. That's more than any other team.

One team is from the American League, and the other is from the National League. The first team to win four games in the series wins the trophy.

The 2016 World Series was amazing! The Chicago Cubs played the Cleveland Indians. The Cubs hadn't won a World Series in 108 years.

They had not even played in a World Series since 1945!

After game six, each team had won three games. The winner of game seven would win the series. More than 40 million people tuned in to watch the game on TV.

Even though game seven was in Cleveland, fans in Chicago crowded into bars and restaurants near Wrigley Field, the Cubs' home ballpark. People milled around in the streets chanting, "Go, Cubs, go!" The game lasted for more than four and a half hours. It ended well after midnight. The Cubs won, 8 to 7!

This Chicago Cubs fan is showing his ticket for the 1945 World Series. He waited a long time for his team to win!

The next morning, five million cheering people flooded into Chicago. They drove around honking their horns. They set off fireworks, hugged, and danced. Then everyone lined the streets to watch a parade honoring their team. It was one of the best World Series ever!

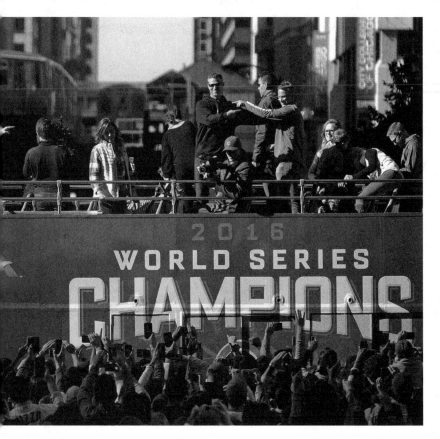

All-American Girls Professional Baseball League

In 1943, the United States was in the middle of World War II. Many men, including baseball players, had gone off to war. Without great players, baseball was becoming less popular.

Women had played baseball since the 1800s, but there were no professional women's leagues. To keep the spirit of baseball alive, the owner of the Chicago Cubs formed a professional women's baseball league. Hundreds of women tried out for positions on the teams.

The women were skillful athletes who

played hard and obeyed the rules of baseball. They also followed rules about how to
dress and act. They couldn't wear pants,
have very short hair, or go without lipstick.
And most of all, they weren't allowed to
"talk tough."

For eleven years, more than 600 women
played professional baseball. Over time the
crowds got smaller, and the league ended
in 1954. Many women who played said that
those were the best years of their lives.

3

The Great
Jackie Robinson

Jackie Robinson was born in Georgia in 1919. His grandparents had been slaves, and the family were poor farmers. No one could have guessed that this African American baby would grow up to change the history of baseball. But Jackie didn't just change baseball; he helped change the way many people thought about equal rights and freedom.

When Jackie was a baby, his father left the family and never returned. Jackie's mother, Mallie, took her children to live in Pasadena, California, to be close to her brothers. She worked long, hard hours cooking and cleaning for other people to support the family.

This photo from around 1925 shows Mallie Robinson and her children—Mack, Jackie, Edgar, Willa Mae, and Frank.

Mallie was able to save enough money to buy a house on Pepper Street in Pasadena. Even though some people didn't want a black family in the neighborhood, Jackie and his three older brothers and sister were happy growing up there.

Jackie's Early Years

While Mallie worked, Jackie's sister, Willa Mae, took care of him. Willa Mae was only a few years older, but she acted like a mother to her little brother. Every day, she brought Jackie to school with her. He sat alone in the sandbox and played while Willa Mae looked out of the classroom window to check on him.

If it rained, Jackie waited for her in the kindergarten room.

When he got older, Jackie was the leader of the Pepper Street Gang. He and his friends played pranks, stole golf balls from a golf course, and shoplifted from stores. Before the kids got into serious trouble, the Reverend Karl Downs reached out to help Jackie. He became the father Jackie never had.

A Gifted Athlete

Jackie looked up to his older brother Mack, a strong athlete. Mack was so good that he won a silver medal in the 200-meter dash in the 1936 Olympics in Berlin, Germany. Jackie hoped that someday he could be in the Olympics like Mack. In high school, he was outstanding in baseball, football, basketball, track, and tennis.

When Jackie was in college, newspapers had stories about what a great athlete he was. There seemed to be almost

Mack Robinson

no sport that he couldn't play. But Jackie knew there was no hope of his playing professional football, basketball, or Major League Baseball. They were for white players only. Black baseball players played on all-black teams in the Negro Leagues.

At this time, African Americans were called Negroes.

Jackie's favorite sport was football.

African American soldiers had their own units. They didn't train with white soldiers.

When World War II began, Jackie, like many young men, joined the army. While he was in the army, Jackie met a soldier who had played for the Negro Leagues. His new friend thought that after the war, Jackie should try out for a baseball team called the Kansas City Monarchs. When the war ended, Jackie signed with the Monarchs.

Jackie's Career Begins

African Americans had played on their own baseball teams since the 1800s.

These Negro League fans gathered for a game at Forbes Field in Pittsburgh.

When Jackie played in the 1940s, there were 200 teams. They played all over the country and had their own championship.

The Negro Leagues ended in the 1950s

The players didn't make much money. Sometimes they had to eat beside the road because no restaurant would serve them. Sometimes they had to sleep in their buses because no motel would let them stay. And sometimes the men couldn't use the restrooms because they were for white people only.

Jackie's Big Move

Branch Rickey was the president of the Brooklyn Dodgers in the 1940s. He was worried that the Dodgers had not been winning enough games. Branch knew he needed to build up the team. When the Monarchs played in Chicago, a Dodger

Branch Rickey and Jackie Robinson

scout saw Jackie and thought he had something special.

Branch Rickey took a chance and asked Jackie to join the Dodgers. Jackie couldn't believe it! This would make him the only black Major League Baseball player.

Branch knew a lot of people wouldn't want a black player on his team. He asked Jackie what he would do if people called him names or treated him badly. Jackie promised to stay calm and not lose his temper or fight back.

That was just what Branch wanted to hear. "I want a player who's got the guts *not* to fight back," he said. Jackie was set to become a Brooklyn Dodger.

Branch and Jackie were so close that when Branch died, Jackie said it was like losing a father.

On the Team

The first thing Branch did was to send Jackie to a minor league team called the Montreal Royals to get more training. Jackie played with them for a year.

Jackie and his wife, Rachel, had begun a family. When Branch thought it was

time for him to join the Dodgers, Jackie
was ready.

Jackie Jr.

Jackie met Rachel in college.
They had a happy family life with
their three children.

Jackie and the Dodgers

On April 15, 1947, Jackie Robinson became one of the first black players on a Major League team. He started as a first baseman. Life on and off the baseball field was really hard. Some fans screamed abuse at him. They threw things on the field, hoping to hit him.

Threats came in the mail, saying his wife and children would be killed. Players on other teams and even some of his own

teammates stepped on him with their cleats or threw balls at his head.

Things were especially bad whenever the Dodgers played against the Philadelphia Phillies. In one game, some players held up their bats like guns and pretended to shoot at him. Jackie later said he almost cracked under the stress, but he never lost his temper.

Jackie and Pee Wee

Pee Wee Reese was the shortstop for the Dodgers. The other players had a lot of respect for him. Some of Jackie's teammates sent around a letter that said they didn't want to play with a black man. Pee Wee refused to sign.

One day when the fans yelled abuse at Jackie, Pee Wee walked across the field, put his hand on Jackie's shoulder, and talked to him a while. Pee Wee showed everyone that he stood with Jackie.

Jackie Robinson and Pee Wee Reese

Jackie and Pee Wee became good friends. Today there's a statue of them next to the minor league ballpark in Coney Island in Brooklyn. Pee Wee has his arm around Jackie's shoulder.

Jackie Keeps His Promise

Jackie always kept his word to Branch. He didn't fight back. Slowly, people began to respect and admire him for his great playing and the way he acted. The Dodgers began to win many more games, and people sent fan letters about Jackie. In the years that followed, other teams also began signing great black players.

Jackie Wins

In 1947, Jackie won the first Rookie of the Year award for being the best new MLB player. Today this prize is called the Jackie Robinson Award.

A rookie is someone new to a job.

In 1949, Jackie had the most hits in the National League. He was named the Most Valuable Player.

Jackie played with the Dodgers for ten years. He was a six-time All-Star and the highest-paid player the team had ever had. Jackie had become a hero to the American people.

In 1950, he even starred in a movie about his life.

After he retired, Jackie became a businessman and worked for civil rights causes. In 1962, he was voted into the National Baseball Hall of Fame. The Hall of Fame is in Cooperstown, New York, and highlights the best baseball players in history. Jackie was the first black player to get this honor.

Jackie died in 1972. Every year on April 15, the day Jackie played his first game for the Dodgers, all MLB players celebrate Jackie Robinson Day. Jackie always wore number 42, so on Jackie Robinson Day, every player wears number 42.

Dem Bums Move!

Brooklyn Dodgers fans loved their team. From 1913 to 1957, people all over the city rushed to Ebbets Field in Brooklyn to see the Dodgers play. The fans called their team "dem bums."

The Dodgers were the heart of Brooklyn. At this time, people came from all over the world to live in Brooklyn. They joined together to cheer for their home team.

In 1957, the Dodgers played their last game in Brooklyn. They were moving to Los Angeles to become the Los Angeles Dodgers. After the last game, many fans stayed in the stands crying. Three years later, a band played music at Ebbets Field as a wrecking crew took down the stadium.

4

National Baseball Hall of Fame

Every year about 300,000 baseball fans head to the National Baseball Hall of Fame and Museum in Cooperstown, New York. It's the best place in the country to learn about the history of baseball and the greatest baseball players.

The Baseball Hall of Fame chose its first members in 1936. Today there are 317 members. They include MLB players, team managers, umpires, and owners. They also have great players from the Negro Leagues.

A group of baseball experts chooses new members every year. To get into the Hall of Fame, baseball players must have played in the Major Leagues for ten years and been retired for five years or more. They are chosen based on how well they played, their sportsmanship, and how much they helped their teams.

Jackie holds up his Hall of Fame plaque in 1962.

What Makes a Great Player?

Baseball players need to be fit enough to play lots of games without much rest in between. Except for starting pitchers who take three to five days off, most players only get a day off every ten days.

Experts have tested baseball players' eyes and say that almost all of them have perfect 20/20 vision or better. This explains why some players can tell the spin of a ball almost the second a pitcher throws it from sixty feet and six inches away.

Barry Bonds is supposed to have had the best eyesight of all the baseball players ever tested.

Great players have great focus. They can tune out noise from the stands. Ted Williams, one of the best batters ever, said he was so focused when he batted, home plate was the quietest place on earth.

Gifted players have very fast reaction times. When a ball comes toward them at ninety miles per hour, they have less than a tenth of a second to react. Even the best batters only hit the ball three times out of ten!

Ted Williams was the last player to average four hits in every ten tries for a whole season.

It's super hard to be chosen for an MLB team. Of all the players who dream of an MLB career, only a few ever make it. And only about five out of every one hundred players make the Hall of Fame!

Let's hit a home run and meet some outstanding Hall of Famers!

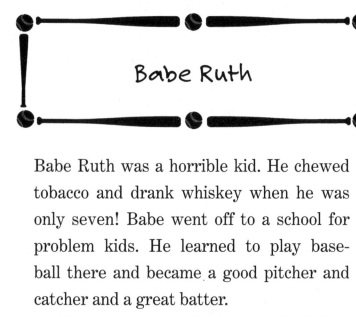

Babe Ruth

Babe Ruth was a horrible kid. He chewed tobacco and drank whiskey when he was only seven! Babe went off to a school for problem kids. He learned to play baseball there and became a good pitcher and catcher and a great batter.

Babe played for the Boston Red Sox, New York Yankees, and Boston Braves. His best year was 1927, when he hit sixty home runs. Babe played for twenty-two seasons and hit 714 home runs.

People often saw Babe walking down the street wearing huge fur coats and smoking

big cigars. After he died, his coffin lay in Yankee Stadium for two days. One hundred thousand fans came to say goodbye to this baseball legend.

Satchel Paige

Leroy "Satchel" Paige's nickname came from the suitcases, or satchels, he carried while working at a train station when he was a kid. When he was caught stealing, Satchel went to a school for problem kids. Like Babe Ruth, Satchel learned baseball there, especially how to pitch.

Satchel first played for the Negro Leagues. In 1947, on his forty-second birthday, he joined the Cleveland Indians. Satchel was the oldest rookie ever! He clowned around on the field a lot. He was famous for his fastballs. He called his favorite pitch the bee ball because he said it made a buzzing sound. Ted Williams said Satchel was the greatest pitcher in baseball.

Satchel retired in 1953. But at age fifty-nine, he pitched one more game, becoming the oldest person ever in the MLB. He really loved baseball, and once said, "I ain't ever had a job. I just always played baseball."

Joe DiMaggio

Some sportswriters say that Joe DiMaggio was the great baseball player ever. Joe's parents came from Italy. To feed his eight children, Joe's father worked as a fisherman. Joe and his friends played baseball in a parking lot for milk wagons. They used rocks for bases and patched their baseballs with bicycle tape.

Joe played his entire career with the New York Yankees. He was a fantastic hitter, a great base runner, and a skilled center fielder. Joe helped the Yankees win nine World Series.

Joe was voted the American League's Most Valuable Player three times. He is still famous for the longest hitting streak in MLB history—fifty-six games in a row. He retired with 361 home runs.

After Joe retired, he raised millions of dollars for a children's hospital in Florida. He was on TV and radio a lot, and there were movies and books about him. When he died, President Bill Clinton said that Joe had been one of America's most beloved heroes.

Mickey Mantle

Mickey Mantle's dad, Mutt, taught him to play baseball. He made his son practice switch hitting so he could bat both right- and left-handed.

Mickey played for the New York Yankees. He hit one of the longest home runs ever—565 feet. The ball flew out of the stadium into someone's backyard! Today you can see Mickey's ball and bat at the Baseball Hall of Fame. Mickey played in twelve World Series, hitting a record eighteen home runs.

Sadly, Mutt died before Mickey became

famous. He never knew that his son turned out to be one of the best baseball players in history.

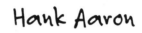

Hank Aaron

Hank was a poor black kid from Alabama. He once heard Jackie Robinson give a speech and vowed to become a baseball player, too.

Hank joined the Negro Leagues and was known as a powerful batter and infielder. In 1954, he started playing for the Milwaukee Braves, an MLB club that later became the Atlanta Braves. Sometimes people in the stands called him names and sent him threatening letters, just as they had with Jackie Robinson.

In 1974, Hank smashed Babe Ruth's

record with his 715th home run. In 1976, when he retired, Hank had hit a total of 755 home runs!

His record stood for thirty-one years, until Barry Bonds broke it. Every year, the MLB gives the Hank Aaron Award to the best hitter from each league.

Roberto Clemente

Roberto came from a poor family in Puerto Rico. He was the first Latino player in the Hall of Fame. Roberto was a great outfielder with a powerful arm. He could throw a ball more than 400 feet! Roberto was also a talented batter, with over 3,000 career hits.

Roberto always helped people, especially poor Puerto Rican kids who wanted to play baseball. In 1972, a terrible earthquake hit Nicaragua. Roberto raised money to fly supplies to the victims. Roberto's plane crashed into the ocean, killing everyone on board. He was only thirty-eight years old.

Even though it usually takes five years after a player retires to get into the Hall of Fame, Roberto Clemente became a member of the Baseball Hall of Fame just one year later. Today, the Roberto Clemente Award is given each year to the MLB player who helps his community and shows the most sportsmanship.

Pedro Martinez

Pedro grew up in the Dominican Republic. He and his five sisters and brothers lived in a one-room house with a dirt floor and tin roof.

Pedro's father and brothers were great ball players, too. But the family was so poor that Pedro couldn't always afford baseballs. Sometimes he used oranges, rolled-up socks, or the heads of his sisters' dolls. When he was thirteen, Pedro could throw a ball eighty miles per hour!

Pedro began pitching with the Los Angeles Dodgers in 1992. He went on to star with four other MLB teams, including the Boston Red Sox. His fastballs clocked in at 100 miles per hour. In 1999, he struck out 313 players and had twenty-three wins. Pedro won the Cy Young Award, given to the best pitcher in each league, three times.

By 2011, Pedro was in pain from years of pitching. He retired, wrote a book about his life, and has been on TV as a baseball commentator. Not bad for a boy who practiced with oranges!

Rally caps

5

Chewing Gum, Balls, and Bats

Baseball players often follow rituals for good luck. If a team is behind, players will sometimes put on their "rally caps." This means they turn their hats inside out and backward or wear them in other crazy ways. It's supposed to help them win.

Some players eat the same food every time they play. Wade Boggs, a Hall of Fame third baseman, ate a chicken dinner before every game. He said it gave him strength to hit the ball hard. Wade ate so much chicken that his teammates nicknamed him Chicken Man.

Elliot Johnson always chews watermelon gum when he bats. He switches to grape gum when he's in the field. Turk Wendell, an MLB pitcher, chewed licorice and then brushed his teeth between each inning.

Other players perform special routines. David Ortiz, for example, always spit into his glove and clapped his hands together before he batted.

Players also believe that using certain bats and gloves brings them good luck. Before an umpire starts the game by yelling "Play ball!" they take their bats and gloves to the dugout. Many players won't let anyone else touch their equipment.

Bats

MLB players have strong feelings about their bats. They use wooden ones and rub the handles with pine tar to keep their hands from slipping.

Many players hit balls that go 80 miles an hour.

Batters always try to hit the ball on their bat's *sweet spot*. The sweet spot is about four to six inches up on the thickest part of the bat. When a player hits the ball on its sweet spot, the bat doesn't vibrate. This makes the hit more powerful.

Players almost never let anyone else use their bats. Some kiss the bats before a game or give them nicknames. The pitcher R. A. Dickey named one of

93

his bats Orcrist the Goblin Cleaver. Go figure!

Ichiro Suzuki's Case

Ichiro Suzuki is a star hitter from Japan who has played for three MLB teams. Ichiro has beautiful black bats with his name printed on them in fancy letters. He takes great care of them and thinks a good player respects his equipment.

Ichiro believes his bats hit better when they are dry. To keep moisture from getting to them, he stores the bats in a special black case. Ichiro carries his batting case with him everywhere he goes.

After a game, he cleans his bats carefully and carries them to the clubhouse

A special craftsman in Japan makes Ichiro's bats and gloves by hand.

to put them back in the case. Once, Ichiro threw a bat down after striking out. He felt so bad that he wrote a letter to the bat maker, saying how sorry he was.

Ted Williams said he treated his bats like babies.

Ted Williams often went to the factory in Kentucky where his bats were made. He liked to choose the perfect pieces of wood for them. He wanted bats that weighed exactly thirty-three ounces, and he weighed them constantly.

Ted spent time rubbing his bats back and forth over a bone. This made the wood fibers bond closer together so the bats became lighter, harder, and more powerful.

Glove Love

Fielders depend on gloves to protect their hands. They have their own special ways of breaking them in. Alex Rodriguez, for example, would put his in the freezer overnight. He said it made them fit better. He also lathered his gloves with shaving cream!

Yogi Berra, like all catchers, used a special catcher's mitt with extra padding.

Other players dunk their gloves in water, beat them with little mallets, or tie them up and put them under their mattresses for several weeks.

When players use a glove for a while, it begins to mold itself to fit their hands. They think that when someone else has put a hand in their glove, it can change its shape. Even a small change can throw them off their game. Roberto Alomar, a second baseman, once charged through the clubhouse yelling, "Who touched my glove? Someone put his hand in my glove. *Who* was it?"

Risking His Life

On October 17, 1989, the Oakland Athletics and the San Francisco Giants were about to play the third game of the World

Series. Suddenly Mike Gallego and his Oakland Athletics teammates felt the earth shaking.

They were afraid the locker room ceiling was going to collapse. The men raced for the door as the lights went out. Mike was halfway to safety in the parking lot when he thought about his glove! He just couldn't leave it behind. Mike raced back in and looked around the dark room until he found it. Then he ran out again.

The earthquake killed 63 people and injured more than 3,000.

Not many people would risk their life for a glove. But not all people are baseball players. One word of advice if you ever meet a Major League Baseball player: don't touch his glove or his bat!

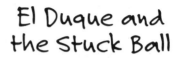

El Duque and the Stuck Ball

In 1999, Orlando "El Duque" Hernandez was pitching for the New York Yankees. A runner was headed to first base when Orlando caught the ball. He was going to throw it to the first baseman to get the runner out. But he had a big problem. The ball was stuck in his glove!

Thinking quickly, El Duque whipped off his glove and threw it to first baseman Tino Martinez. Tino caught the glove just in time. Since the glove had the ball in it, the runner was out!

6

An Exciting, Wonderful Game

No matter where they are from or the color of their skin, baseball brings people together. When a city's team wins the World Series, all fans cheer and celebrate. And players from all backgrounds can be on the field enjoying a great sport together without anger or hatred.

There are still no women playing for the Major Leagues, but today there are all-women's leagues. Women from around the world compete in the Women's Baseball World Cup. They don't have to wear lipstick, and their hair can be as short or as long as they want it to be.

Japan won the Women's Baseball World Cup in 2016.

A Crazy, Funny Game (Sometimes)

Baseball can sometimes be laugh-out-loud funny. When the Baltimore Orioles had a losing streak in 1988, a radio DJ in Baltimore named Bob Rivers vowed to stay awake playing music until the Orioles won. People carried signs begging the Orioles to win and free poor Bob. Drivers kept their lights on to support him.

Bob ate lots of pizza and dozed off while the music played. He lasted eleven days, and then the Orioles won! Bob went home and fell into bed. The next day the Orioles lost again.

In 1999, New York Mets manager Bobby Valentine got thrown out of a game by the umpire. He put on a hat, glasses, and a false mustache and sneaked back into the dugout. It didn't work. Bobby got caught and was fined and suspended for two games.

In 2007, Lou Piniella, manager of the Chicago Cubs, got so angry at an umpire's call that he threw his hat on the ground. Then he kicked it all over the field! The umpire tossed Lou out. But then all the fans threw their hats on the field to show support for Lou. The grounds crew had a big job getting the field cleaned up!

Lou Piniella

Bernie Williams and Derek Jeter

It's Healthy

People stay fit by playing baseball. The exercise they get gives them strong legs and good balance. Playing ball on sunny days is also a good way to soak up vitamin D that helps keep your bones strong. Since running burns a lot of calories, baseball is also good for a healthy weight. So play baseball and stay healthy!

Teammates and Friends

Bryce Harper and Joey Gallo are young pro players on different teams. They've been friends since their Little League days in Las Vegas, Nevada. Bryce and Joey learned back then that even though they sometimes played against each other, they could be friends. They are still friends today.

Baseball is really about fun, friendship, and learning how to be a good sport. You don't have to be a great player. Work hard and play hard. As the famous catcher Yogi Berra once said, "I tell kids, somebody's got to win, somebody's got to lose. Just don't fight about it. Just try to get better."

Doing More Research

There's a lot more you can learn about baseball. The fun of research is seeing how many different sources you can explore.

Books

Most libraries and bookstores have books about baseball.

Here are some things to remember when you're using books for research:

1. You don't have to read the whole book. Check the table of contents and the index to find the topics you're interested in.

2. Write down the name of the book.

When you take notes, make sure you write down the name of the book in your notebook so you can find it again.

3. Never copy exactly from a book.

When you learn something new from a book, put it in your own words.

4. Make sure the book is <u>nonfiction</u>.

Some books tell make-believe stories about baseball. Make-believe stories are called *fiction*. They're fun to read, but not good for research.

Research books have facts and tell true stories. They are called *nonfiction*. A librarian or teacher can help you make sure the books you use for research are nonfiction.

Here are some good nonfiction books about Jackie Robinson and baseball:

- *Baseball* (DK Eyewitness) by James Buckley
- *Baseball: How It Works* by David Dreier
- *The Everything Kids' Baseball Book* by Greg Jacobs
- *My First Book of Baseball: A Rookie Book* by the editors of *Sports Illustrated*
- *Who Was Jackie Robinson?* by Gail Herman

Museums

Many museums can help you learn more about baseball.

When you go to a museum:

1. Be sure to take your notebook!
Write down anything that catches your interest. Draw pictures, too!

2. Ask questions.
There are almost always people at museums who can help you find what you're looking for.

3. Check the calendar.
Many museums have special events and activities just for kids!

Here are some museums with exhibits about baseball:

- Babe Ruth Birthplace and Museum (Baltimore)
- Louisville Slugger Museum & Factory (Louisville, Kentucky)
- National Baseball Hall of Fame and Museum (Cooperstown, New York)
- Negro Leagues Baseball Museum (Kansas City, Missouri)
- Ted Williams Museum and Hitters Hall of Fame (St. Petersburg, Florida)
- World of Little League Museum (Williamsport, Pennsylvania)

The Internet

Many websites have lots of facts about baseball. Some also have games and activities that can help make learning about it even more fun.

Ask your teacher or your parents to help you find more websites like these:

- coolfactsforkids.com/baseball-facts-for -kids
- ducksters.com/sports/jackie_robinson .php
- factmonster.com/sports/baseball
- factmonster.com/negro-league-baseball -history-players
- kidskonnect.com/sports/baseball

Keywords

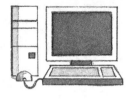

Baseball is a very broad topic. When you search the Internet, you may need to use more specific keywords to find the information you're looking for.

Here are some words and terms that may help narrow down your search.

American League	hit (baseball)
baseball umpire	home run
base running	infield
bases	inning
batter	Jackie Robinson
catcher	National League
double play	Negro Leagues
fielding	outfield
force out	pitcher
foul ball	strikeout

Selected Bibliography

- Bryant, Howard. *Legends: The Best Players, Games, and Teams in Baseball.* New York: Philomel, 2015.

- Kahn, Roger. *The Boys of Summer.* New York: Harper & Row, 1972.

- Robinson, Jackie, and Alfred Duckett. *I Never Had It Made.* New York: Putnam, 1972.

- Schumacher, Chuck. *How to Play Baseball: A Parent's Role in Their Child's Journey.* New York: Dunham, 2014.

- Tygiel, Jules. *Baseball's Great Experiment: Jackie Robinson and His Legacy.* New York: Oxford University Press, 1983.

Index

**Have you read the adventure that
matches up with this book?
Don't miss**

Magic Tree House® #29

A Big Day for Baseball

Jack and Annie go back in time to a ball
game in 1940s Brooklyn, New York. Does
Morgan's magical plan for them involve . . .
Jackie Robinson?

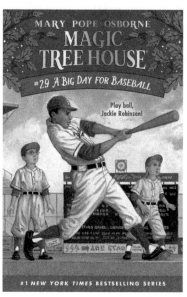

YOU'LL LOVE FINDING OUT THE FACTS BEHIND THE FICTION IN

Magic Tree House® Fact Tracker

Wild West

A NONFICTION COMPANION TO
Ghost Town at Sundown

It's Jack and Annie's very own guide to
America's Old West.

Coming in January 2018!

Magic Tree House®

Magic Tree House®
Merlin Missions

Magic Tree House®
Super Edition

#1: WORLD AT WAR, 1944

Magic Tree House®
Fact Trackers

DINOSAURS
KNIGHTS AND CASTLES
MUMMIES AND PYRAMIDS
PIRATES
RAIN FORESTS
SPACE
TITANIC
TWISTERS AND OTHER TERRIBLE STORMS
DOLPHINS AND SHARKS
ANCIENT GREECE AND THE OLYMPICS
AMERICAN REVOLUTION
SABERTOOTHS AND THE ICE AGE
PILGRIMS
ANCIENT ROME AND POMPEII
TSUNAMIS AND OTHER NATURAL DISASTERS
POLAR BEARS AND THE ARCTIC
SEA MONSTERS
PENGUINS AND ANTARCTICA
LEONARDO DA VINCI
GHOSTS
LEPRECHAUNS AND IRISH FOLKLORE
RAGS AND RICHES: KIDS IN THE TIME OF
   CHARLES DICKENS
SNAKES AND OTHER REPTILES
DOG HEROES
ABRAHAM LINCOLN

PANDAS AND OTHER ENDANGERED SPECIES
HORSE HEROES
HEROES FOR ALL TIMES
SOCCER
NINJAS AND SAMURAI
CHINA: LAND OF THE EMPEROR'S GREAT
   WALL
SHARKS AND OTHER PREDATORS
VIKINGS
DOGSLEDDING AND EXTREME SPORTS
DRAGONS AND MYTHICAL CREATURES
WORLD WAR II
BASEBALL

More Magic Tree House®

GAMES AND PUZZLES FROM THE TREE HOUSE
MAGIC TRICKS FROM THE TREE HOUSE
MY MAGIC TREE HOUSE JOURNAL
MAGIC TREE HOUSE SURVIVAL GUIDE
ANIMAL GAMES AND PUZZLES
MAGIC TREE HOUSE INCREDIBLE FACT BOOK